THE GRIEF POOL

THE GRIEF POOL

Poems by
Jeff Crandall

FIRESTORM
PRESS

ISBN 0-9679824-0-5

First Edition: April, 2000

Cover photograph: *Unrequited Love* by Shelly Corbett
Cover design by Michael Bails

Firestorm Press logo by Michael Bails
Printed on acid-free, recycled paper by Thomson-Shore
Set in Adobe Garamond

10 9 8 7 6 5 4 3 2 1

Firestorm Press
PO Box 94714
Seattle, WA 98124

For Ruth Robinson and Bob Hoover

CONTENTS

Love is a debt. When the bill comes, you pay in grief.

— *Children of God*, Mary Doria Russell

PROLOGUE

Mario "Duke" Duque
1957 — 1997

NAMES

If you knew him as *Junior,* you're family.
You know he's as East Coast crass as Baltimore gets,
know he was born in Colombia — a spirit too free for this world.
You worried about him during the sixties,
called often when he settled in Seattle.
Your love for him is pained, confused,
wordless in its depth.

If you knew him as *Buck*, you're a client.
You know the magic of his hands, the pleasures
he gave, his efficiency with bills. You know
shampoo is a euphemism and
bought it, discreetly, often. I've seen you
occasionally, at parties, stopping by
at two in the morning, red-eyed, slurred.
You weren't at the wake.

If you knew him as *Duke*, as I did, you met him
at the nude beach, wondered briefly
what this odd little man could possibly offer
with his body-builder's body and tight goatee.
You were charmed by his sheer honesty, marveled
at his lack of subtext, his embrace
of the underworld. You enjoyed those brash
arguments. He taught you anger
was merely a moth tickling your nose. You loved him
as a lover, a kind of funny mentor, a magical imp.

If you called him *Sweetheart,* your name is Bill. You were
his one lasting love, a muscled hummingbird of activity

grounding a relationship so open and giving
it astounded everyone. You spoiled him
with roses and leather and love and
died of AIDS in his arms.

If you called him *Mario,* you knew him through the hippie days,
the hitchhiking and communes, his thriving
at pottery, his leaving art school.
He was a pole in the planet of your life, the brother
you never had, the man who showed you what
living was, what it meant to take life by the balls
and squeeze. You'd do anything for him — *anything* — even
burn his bones, scatter his ashes, liquidate
everything he ever owned if he asked you.
And he did.

THE MAN IN ROOM 34

White tape ripping at his papery skin,
the IV catheter tugging wrong, he
twists in the dark like a pulled stitch. Alone,

under the bone pop, knuckled fingers feel
his face, his chest, crawl the clean air toward
the shade pull's dull plumb, which lightly bobs here

and there — at last — he catches it. The cord
tugged, in little jerks, with less strength than fear,
less faith than bladed pain — and a breath, and

a breath — he will not let go — until one
corner lifts off the sill. From this dead end
view, the now-just-rising, cold and blurred sun

angles in. He falls back, eyes tight. Alive,
yes, in the brief light of one more reprieve.

PATIENT

8:30 P.M, No one told me they lock this place. I press
the delivery door buzzer. Three floors up,
I'm surprised by the dim room filled with people.
The only place left on the crowded couch is kept by a small
pile of papers I lift and hold in my lap as I squeeze in.
An old friend I've never known is telling how he met
his wife while he and Duke hitchhiked to California in the '70's.
Ruth fills in laughable details from her side.
I am grossly uncomfortable. I do not share this history.
I don't even know what I'm holding: a cross-
word puzzle, Reader's Digest and photocopied pages titled
PREPARING FOR APPROACHING DEATH

Mm.

Is this what we're doing? Is this how you're
supposed to do it? With smiles, with easy
tales and an upbeat attitude, a rush to help
the nurse lift him comfortably upright, a dash
down the hall for another glass of ice, another
cherry jello, infinite
patience as the shaking bones of his hands
take whole minutes to lift the glass to his lips,
patience as his flesh recedes, leaving the skin
draped over roots of his collarbone where
the sweetly-salted bath water collects in pools,
as the lucidity of who you are after eleven years

sinks in and he says *Where did* you *come from?*
I don't think so. To prepare for
approaching death

I need crockery, a concrete room, a solid wall
to hurl cups like epithets. I need
bats and hammers, blue willow tureens
and cheap, thick china to smash and smash,
a deep-walled room where I can scream and rip
the stuffing out of a mattress, a room
far from the syrup of pity, where one bare bulb
spits and fizzes on a frayed wire
dripping my face with rheumy light
as deep, yellow and fading as his eyes.

LANDSCAPES

This happened to me: leaving my friend's hospice room
to walk his best dog in the world from the third floor
to the elevator where two women talking already pressed
the down button and the doors opened like a yawn and we got
in me the dog two women the elevator stopped one floor down
and a nurse — I think she was a nurse she was dressed like us
I think she had a name tag — looked at us with a look that said
These are the only words I am able to say and said
"Would you mind taking the next elevator down?" no one
had ever said that to any of us before and we stood
in the elevator with the door open looking at her until she
repeated the question "Would you mind . . ." so polite we
couldn't understand the stricken look on her face we
stepped out of the elevator the two women first then
the dog then me I figured someone must be afraid
of other people perhaps claustrophobic or maybe not
wanting to be seen by strangers this gentle nurse I
stepped aside looked away for a convenient time turned
to see the quilt on the gurney a quilt of squares as if
all the red-rimmed glory of sunset had been pixilated
or flying above a farmer's landscape one plot lavender
the next crimson tulips August wheat alfalfa surrounded
by ochres of rich upturned earth daffodils and corn husks
the whole brilliant sheet of it rolling over the hills that some-
how formed the shape of somebody horizontally heading
head first into the elevator and descending
and that quilt covering even his face.

HELP

1. Menu

The laborious, lugubrious effort of breakfast
has proved too much. The raising of the head,
the shoulders and torso into unsupporting air,
the burning wrench of the liver, the body's
torque, creak and pop of legs
dragged to the bed edge, lowered, dangling over its
abyss, the clench and grimace *(my trooper, my superman)*
into the wheelchair wheeled down the long hall
to the dining room where *soup?* is cream of
what? spoonful of mashed
this one or that one? a little too liquid, a little
of this? has drained the remaining strength
the last two cubes of jello gave you. Tonight we'll dine
bedside, half
awake. *(Please,*
just one more bite?)
We've got popsicles dripping with juice, succulent
chunks of watermelon, mashed potatoes smothered in smooth,
easy gravy. We've chilled compotes and puddings, milkshakes
melding malt and chocolate, coconut and papaya, *Duke,*
we've got anything, anything *you want.*

2. Relief

Now we know he will not rise from this bed
alone again. We know two bites of food will not sustain
his bones two days. Still,
we flutter about, frantic as doves,

startling into flight at his every weak utterance —
"I need to pee,"
and the word *privacy* gongs through our minds
as we, who so desperately need to do
something, anything
file out when the nurse comes in.
I'm closing the door when she looks at me and asks,
"Can you help?"

Helplessness

is what's killing me. I've never done this. I'm afraid
to even feed him ice, afraid he'll choke, not knowing
how to raise a frail man higher on the bed without pain,
not knowing when it's rude to be here, when I should leave him.
The nurse places my hand — *here* and
here — as we ease him up between us, slide
his garments and underwear down.
I help her position the outsized container

at his groin, so that the hard plastic won't abrade.
(Who made these evil things?) As always, Duke takes his time.
When he finally murmurs, "Okay," the syllables barely audible,
we ease him back down, readjust his clothes, the sheet,

the quilt. The nurse takes the container
with its minim of dark, ochre liquid
to the bathroom. Duke is already asleep.

I do not think about what I've just done.
I open the door
and let the others in.

16

What Does a Dog Know

About death? About love? Nothing
eased me more that day than a noon walk,
a wire-haired joke of a Dachshund
waddling away from the antiseptic silence

of the hospice. His joy conjured the fusty
smuts at the roots of trash cans,
a competition of foreign canine urea,
trail of cat, rabbit, finch. I was content

to explore every corner mailbox, every crenellated hedge
perhaps for hours. We walked
one block, two. I knew the arboretum's
dog-run barks and dogwood lanes would draw him in,

but Jazz sniffed at a juniper — peed — tugged me
back two blocks to that glass door. Inside
he strained toward the elevator, nose to the closed
steel mouth as the lights counted down. We rose

to its chime, to the third floor where
he pulled me down the long hall, into Room 34,
to the foot of a bed scrubbed clean
of any human scent, to a man

stuck in a slumber of knives. A blanket lay curled
on the floor by the wall but he dropped to the cool tile
beside the bed like a sack of despair,
head on his paws, looking up.

BREAK

"Has difficulty telling friends he doesn't want visitors."
 — *chart entry*

After three days of all of us trying
to break your mother's vigil for more
than a four-minute cigarette, Rick
convinced her to go for a drive.
I was helping a friend take his two
young boys to the movies. Dennis'
dog kept him delayed. Andrew was picking up Scott,
Patrick painting a landscape due Monday,
Bruce singing with the chorus. We knew, all of us, later,
when you played your little trick with the breathing
that sent Bob out of the room and down the hall
to the nurses' station, you finally figured out
how to be alone.

I've seen the effort, the concentration it takes —
dying, moderating
the pain in your shoulder with
the burning in your gut, keeping track of
time, of whose voice is in the room, what
movie they're watching. The constant
decisions: to sleep, drink, pee,
wake, speak, drink,
and on and on.
And every few minutes another
Pill? Pillow? Pain? Do you feel

18

pain? Do you want to sit
up? Cold? Your feet? Your head? Your shirt?
Where is the peace to be found
in the bald repetitions of
I love you.

       Alone,
in your room at last, like you hadn't been for weeks,
you heard the overhead fan click off,
the wind outside,
found the time
to do what you've needed to do for days.
You took a long, deep sigh.
And then you died.

Two Hours Since You Died

5.

I can't bear to hug you anymore, yet here
I've gone all tactile while your friends
still have words. No one
touches anyone, as if each skin
were cool as yours. We sit in our chairs,
stuffed knee to knee on the couch in this
anteroom and I'm reaching out with everything I've got
and no one's taking my hand.
Whatever it is we're supposed to be doing
we're not doing it right because sitting here all calm and quiet
I just want to scream. We're all waiting for your mother to

4.

return, to hear the news,
to understand her son has become
body. One by one

we've said our tight-throated goodbyes.
And what am I supposed to say to you
I didn't when you were alive? Yesterday.

Years ago.
You knew this was the only way
the tumor on your liver would ever stop growing.

Now you are cast in wax, a perfect statue. Your skin
cool and golden, draped over you like robes
of the fasting Buddha. This is

painless. Talking
stops, and suddenly everyone has somewhere else to be,
the lunchroom, bathroom, hallway, leaving

Bruce and I

    3.

on the couch, our eyes red-rimmed,
reaching out our arms like
dammit I need to be held — we
hold each other, our eyes
stones of pain thrown into the same sea,
our pooling love for you having
nowhere else to go. We

kiss

— oh,
if I could have stayed in that moment
for months, until the first smooth sheets
of fall rain fell and fell,
the simple, easy understanding of love
clasping us together, as if

    2.

on the way from here to there,
Duke,
you old ghost,
you cast one last spell.
Were you laughing?

1.

Steps in the hall bring us back
to death.

Your mother now
in the other room,

in other tears.
We go to her —

our only gift
the slow enclosure

of our warm, empty arms.

Avoiding the Undertaker
— *for Ruth*

Sun has set. Your son's friends have turned to doves
and flown home to mourn in their own silences.
A bad man is coming to take your son's body away.

Now we must leave, before he snatches our souls.
Now we must leave because what comes next is unbearable,
and you have borne so much already. We leave Bob alone

to barter your son's passage as we slip into the night,
into my blue car and drive far away. I know a little restaurant
where love once bloomed and — oh, anyway, the food is good.

"He always remembered me," you said,
"My birthday, Mother's Day, Christmas . . ."
Now there is only spaghetti, garlic bread, a sweet wine

that still tastes sour. I cannot convince you to take
more than a bite of dessert and suddenly
it's over. We're driving back through the rain,

down that long hill to the hospice where
a man has left in his great dark car to do his dark work.
We endure the elevator's dull hum, the hall's silence.

How flat and wrinkled his sheets lie.
The air here still breathes of him.
Bob has packed boxes with Mario's shirts, photos,

the last music he heard, the sheaves of unsigned papers.
All that remains are your clothes in the bottom drawers,
the half-finished puzzles, your purse —

you pack these quickly and we lift them into our arms.
And the emptiness of that room is the emptiness in your eyes.
And none of us will ever bend again toward that lovely, rumpled bed.

Death Is a Famous Movie Star

Sultry, scripted, larger than life, someone
we ogle from afar, amazed at how she pulls it off
in film after film. We follow her exploits
fantastic in the tabloids, her shocking
comments on talk shows, the rumors of her
blasphemous palace. She is huge, un-
touchable, godly, acknowledged by all
as the Queen who — yes, my cousin actually
caught a glimpse of.

But to her mother, her maids, her good
friends, Death is just another
plain Jane — they know her
fears and foibles, her shirts and socks
left on the floor, her love of seafood.
They know she's terrified of spiders,
harbors a weakness for Rocky Road and loves
the viola over any other musical instrument.
The men and women who work with Death,
to tell the truth, find her rather routine,
predictable, demanding in her talents,
indifferent to praise. "Goodbye, Death,"
they say, after an all-night shift. "See you tomorrow."

So who am I to enter this hospice
like a gawking tourist, my eyes wide,
agog at Death's efficiencies,
her swiftness and finality,
her easy, familial comforts.

BABBLE

So now you're dead. Dead,
deceased, bereft
of life, dead as a doornail, a phone line,
an engine that won't turn over, dead
still. You are the Late Mario,
passed on, dearly
departed, you've kicked the
goddamn bucket Duke, met
your maker, moved on
to higher ground, you've made
the great escape, like Houdini,
slipped off the chains and out the trap door,
you've made a date with an angel, finally
got your wings *yessiree*. You finally
did it, you're gone, you're *dead*
dead   dead   dead   dead . . . .

*

Here I am
alive. *Alive,*
with its contracted
I HAVE at the end, as in:
"Hooray! I've life." *Life,*
with its big IF in the middle . . .

WHITE SAGE

Blessed
to receive
the last good week with you, I knew you wished
for one last trip to Palm Springs, so we arrived
in hundred-degree heat, excited

and weak. I packed a bag
of patience and found a fabulous heated pool.
We drove our red luxury rental,
dared unmarked backroads promising more desert
than you could endure. You wanted

mountains, so we spiraled up those pink
snaking roads, ascending to the park signs.
You waited in the car while I wandered, returning to explain
sugarleaf and its sweetness. You said,
"Look at that Indian." I don't know why

I stopped, thinking of dementia — of what that means.
We were alone in the parking lot, only
one white truck and — *yes* — there he was —
an Indian with his feathered and skull-capped prayer stick,
his wolf fur and plastic-framed glasses.

He got into his truck and
waited. Not moving. And so
I went over to say *hi*. Yes,
he was a little crazy. Yes, he was a medicine man,
telling me how to soak marijuana buds in vodka

to create an ointment for arthritis. He told me
the healing powers of white sage
taken as a tea. "Not too strong or your face will twitch
like this. And if you burn the white sage
it will clean the air. Burn it and pray. Pray for your Papa.
That your Papa?" I laughed as he motioned to you,
laughed at what your outburst would be
if you heard such an insult! He told me

it grows high up in the mountains.
He opened his glove compartment and gave me a sprig
to offer the bush as a gift before I took any more.
But you got weaker every day.
We looked and looked but never found the bush, stopping

whenever nausea forced its way back up.
And I still have the sprig — here — in my hand,
and I'm praying, Duke — *god I'm praying* —
as your body burns
in the crematorium.

Driving to the Coast, We're Passed by a Gold Hearse

Carrying some body to its next appointment
in the fast lane, no less. I drive west. Ruth, Bob,
silent in their seats. We are each burdened
by the remaindered slag of the body's sorrow.
I can't argue anymore

that memories of friendship are worth any less
than a fruitless hope for one more true embrace.
The windshield wipers give a little scream
with each sweep. I try to recall the last words
I spoke to him. I only remember telling myself

breathe, breathe, breathe
under the thickening hospice light.
Now I will ease my ache into salt fog,
through the low moan of a lighthouse,
knowing only the the rock crag where sea lions bark,

where clean rain rinses the beach logs, where
he wanted his ashes scattered. Ahead,
someone's house has split
into two WIDE LOADS weighting the truckbeds.
Cars pile up behind them. The burning

eyes of brake lights and turn signals
stare and blink. And there it is again —
the hearse — stopped just ahead,
gold flags sagging in the rain,
as we all slow to a halt.

MOTHER
—— *for Ruth*

The hard work began when we reached the beach.
At the very edge of America, standing above the rough grasses,
you looked out over that long finger of rock stretching out
into the Strait of Juan De Fuca and said,

"I'll never make that." You didn't consider
three frantic trips from Baltimore to Seattle to sit
for days with your son in a hospital not knowing
which trip would be your last, or your week-long vigil

by his bed, his every meal, every silence, every two A.M.
murmur until he decided to quietly leave, leaving you
hundreds of photographs, a houseful of goods, a dog, a death
certificate and questions and paperwork.

"You can make it," I said and we eased forward
foothold by foothold, hand in hand, careful to avoid
the low-tide-exposed urchins and starfish, anemones and barnacles.
Slowly, methodically, you moved

from a young marriage in Colombia
to single motherhood in America, in late-forties Baltimore,
barely speaking English, sewing for a living, learning new
foods and verbs. Married an American cheat who left you

a daughter who left you to find herself in the sixties,
lost among love and drugs and destitution. Your one son,
a light of love a continent away in Seattle. Both gone now.
The rocks gave way to yards and yards of mussel beds. We rested.

"I've willed my body to John Hopkins," you said. "I only got
two older sisters. What good's a grave? Maybe a few years
someone puts flowers, then they die too. Graves are forgotten."
"Are those alive?" you asked, looking down

at all the blind, blue-and-black mouths sealed and silent.
"Yes, yes, they're all alive," I said, as their thick shells
held your weight without cracking. You held roses in your hand,
looked ahead to where Bob and Deborah waited with the ashes.

Knowing you would live well into the coming century
you took those next wearisome steps.

What Love Is
— for Bob Hoover

"Oh god please no," I prayed
as Deborah burst out with "Wait, wait, wait —
let me get my camera!" Bob paused,
staring at her, holding two bags of ash
that were once lovers. The incoming tide

lifted like an intake of breath.
Who was this woman
who insisted on following us
through our private procession?
What splintered segment, what odd niche
in Duke's life did she inhabit?

"Just go ahead," I murmured, as she
clucked and rummaged through her bag. He poured
Bill into Mario, Mario into Bill.

Under the click and whir of her insistence, we took
turns pouring ash into the sea, all the while she recited
a litany of babble: "This is my Mario — my sweet
Mario — Mario and Bill — go — go out into the world —
be free — freedom — angels — angels surround us —"

her gift of nonstop talk exposing her grief
like a book torn open by the wind,
only silenced at last, when it came time to hold

each other. Roses
        and lavender
                tossed into the clear sea,
                                    rising
                    and falling away.
            The shock
      of those red petals
               against the soothing
                          sunlit
              water.

All the long walk back
over the mussel beds, the slick
seaweed-covered rocks, along the cliffside
and easy beach, she ladled out her thoughts
like an oddly seasoned stew:

"This is a beautiful day — a perfect day — too much
sun wouldn't have been good — I love the sea — I love
green — sea — green, green sea —
Mother Nature — God bless us —" her voice

fading ahead. I looked at Bob for help, for some
joinder in my silent, angry censure of her.
"We are all doing this out of love," he said.
"— Angels — angels everywhere — "

SISTER

I never knew her, Duke's sister,
the beautiful angel who fled the city
cursed with the voice of God in her head,
who balanced sanity with starvation on a blade
of pure crystal dissolving in her mouth like love,
whose holy mission was to scour the sidewalks for fallen
bracelets, earring backs, the random rhinestones thrown
from the rings of the rich, to toss them into the thick
hand of the pawnshop man and reclaim an hour of her life.
I only heard that she wore survival like a stained vest,
knotted and tattered, the frayed edges
unraveling around her. She died
with too much heaven in her veins and came to rest
in a little black box set in the back of Duke's antique hutch.

As for my sister's ashes — we took her with us,
the three of us in a small blue car and headed farther west
to the coast, into the gathering darkness of clouds.
A bone-knocking wind brought rain
thrown like gravel as we pulled up to the beach
near the sea stacks. The great reaches of sand,
abandoned and desolate, disappearing into the mists,
the once-calm sea a gray boil of gossip and laundry,
concussions of waves hitting the shore like the slap of bad news.

Bob and I took off our shoes,
waded up to our knees,
opened the box.

A burst of dust whirled upward and through us and into the air.
The undulant waves muddied for an instant
and the ash in the water
surged and bloomed and dissipated
and all the little pieces too heavy for flight
settled like coins on the seafloor.

As the last of her children drifted away,
Ruth waited — small and unyielding
on the beach, alone
in the roar and turmoil, the wrack of salt and sea,
clutching the bright red petal of a useless umbrella.

WAKE

The moon's pared down to a nub of a thumbnail.
Earthrise must be beautiful there. Here, in the full
blaze of fall, we're setting down tins and bowls and cutlery.
If *you are what you eat* is true,
we are a remarkably fresh and healthy bunch:
pasta and peppers, whole grain breads home-baked,
silver salmon gleaming with lemon, tarragon, thyme.

Each of us has come to savor and share our portions of him.
To pet his dog who whines and wags his way through the crowd.
To pour out our jokes and stories, conjuring some glowing
holograph out of our laughter, to turn him over in memory
and complete the portrait.

We form a circle around his absence, each of us
holding our plate of sadness, knowing this hollow
echo — in the chest — where it's hard to breathe —
is a hole no love will ever fill. Over the chatter,
the funny mix of memory and mimicry, sadness and silliness,
Bob stands, at last, with his glass of wine,
and calls us all into the empty living room.

SUNFLOWERS, AFTER THE WAKE

Swollen and fat as the bags under my eyes
the sunflowers are indulging their spongy
death: heads hung, petals rotting,
sepals curling back like yellowing wallpaper.

This is the harvest of my last planting —
a flourishing blossom of decay so fragrant
raccoons and rats are finding ways
to plunge their teeth into these seedheads.

I fell them like trees. They topple and thud
on the sod. Like a butcher, I hack
and hack at stems as thick as my wrist,
tossing each boney bit into the binned compost.

I turn these suns under, surrender them
to dirt, to the sloughing cherry leaves, moldy beets
compounded within this mounded earth oven,
the roughage of fall steaming in its own dissolve.

Who knows what good I can reclaim,
what loam — rich and bitter as wisdom —
will settle from this waste, this rot,
this terrible, terrible loss.

THE GRIEF POOL

Cup of coffee. Cigarette. Glazed doughnut.
A woman stands by the planter
outside her office, indulging
in what keeps her going. Across the square,
I sit in front of a low fountain
holding a sackful of nothing.

I've no reason to question the slow death of my friend.
I only need to endure the echoes
and ripples rebounding over water,
the great upwellings breaking into coils,
the one dark leaf nudging along like a rat.
Such weight drags out all manner of loss —

like wrong fish caught in a seine net.
Now I'm missing an aunt long dead, I'm furious
over my father's silences, plunged
into argument with an old lover
I still love. I have nothing
to keep me buoyed

in these waters. I have
bills to pay, phone calls to make,
files to clear and how do I now decide
between wheat or rye at the deli?
How can I begin the unraveling
of cellophane and twist-ties, the complex

undoing required to simply eat?
The woman on break pulls back the door —
sun flashes my eyes. She's left
her cold coffee, stained filter, sweet crumbs.
I cup my bitterness in both hands
and drink deeply.

CHEAP JOY

Pink tag day meant HALF OFF MEN'S SUITS, like us,
barely used. You chose three off the far rack,
pushed me into the changing room, and fussed

over a western jacket fringed in black.
You made me strip to the waist because it
looked *"tooo* sexy!" Copper-lined wool sagged flat

with sleeves too short, but the cream linen fit
so well you launched into an aria that
sent me dashing crimson to my own shirt.

Later you told the cashier I was your
Armani prince. Of course, she loved to flirt
back. I was simply too amazed. Just four

bucks. It was always so easy with you
to skip the movie, walk around the lake
again. You taught me how to rummage, glue

together broken plates and glass to make
an end table's whorled mosaic, paint faux
finish on an old chair, always finding

beauty where others have lost, a rainbow
for every storm. When you spied dishwashing
liquid in "Damaged Goods," an *Ahhh!* poured

out. Shamelessly happy, you grabbed them — dents
and all — ten bottles, loading my arms, yours,
sun-filled, lemony-fresh, 99 cents.

EXECUTOR

Today we arrive with shears and rakes,
break open the garage doors, haul the relics
of your life to the curbside: the old couch,
screen door, half-eaten blankets. We attack
the front yard, rip out small trees dying
for light, whack back the shrubbery, reveal
the fence. We tell ourselves you're at a place
"of greater understanding," knowing you'd raise
holy hell if we ever tried this stunt while you were alive.
Bob pulls up the sickly junipers guarding the back porch,
fulfilling his smiling promise to rip those suckers out
over your dead body. "I love you, Mario," he curses
as the roots release in a shower of dirt and dust.

We all love you, but we don't know how
to accept with grace the spoils of the war you lost.
One by one, we take a towel, a dish,
a parrot from your collection, a picture from the wall.
Here is your knuckle, here your kneecap.
You have rooms and rooms of good taste.
We are all so concerned
for each other that our rummage soon devolves
into a farce of polite deferments: "No,
no. You take it. Really, I couldn't. I have enough I —"
until Bob starts shoving things into our hands shouting
"Take it, dammit — shut up!"

We all want the same thing:
to take the most expensive items you own —

the rings and coins, the French armoire,
television and artwork to the pawn shop.
To purchase back from that bad man your
body, your soul. Carry them to this empty home
and reassemble the Duke we knew: healthy
and hot-tempered, opinionated and loving,
stubborn and irrational. We want it all.

Epilogue

1. Carnus

I am hell's white mouth.
The Gretel oven. I am the fiery-eyed
spider that feeds on the fluids — fats
and acids, oils and plasma, your ducted
tears. I disassemble
the structure of tibia and rib, the skyscraper
spine, the skull's clean bowl. Crusher.
I grind knee caps and teeth alike.
I exhale your last breath.
Thank me.

2. Sorcer

Reduction. Under the pure fire, I stir
and stir the body's alchemy.
What are you, sir?
Carbon and phosphor,
broom and bone,
a sum of other people's memories.
I say, what are you?
An assemblage of salts born in the belly of stars:
calcium, magnesium, potassium.
The body's engine fueled by
pheromone, instinct, hunger.

3. Asphodel

When your friends pour you
            into the ocean
                        to bloom,
                                    at last, in the incoming tide,
                        that cloud of ash — you,
            all you —
shall be
            indistinguishable from the up-
                                                welling sand
                                    churned by the rising
                        plungers and spillers.
    The bits and pieces
            of bone a scattering of
                        broken shells on the seabed . . .

ACKNOWLEDGMENTS

Grateful acknowledgment is given to the following individuals without whose incredible faith, support and generosity this book would not have been possible:

Randy Arnold, Michael Bails, Reba Blissell, Arthur Bremer, Randy Brooks & Ron Towle, Jackson Carter & David York, Miki Church, T. Clear, Joe & Claudia Crandall, Kate Crandall, Ken Crandall & Cheryl Newman-Crandall, Paul Crandall, Victor Crandall, Colette Crosnier & John Beall, Veliere Crump, Rick Davis & Gordon Layman, Diane Daniel, Bruce Ecord & Sid Foutz, Jules Remedios Faye, Claire Garoutte, Linda Hasselstrom, Michele Hasson, Gary Houle, John Kerr, Cheryl Jo Kilts, Marjorie Levy, Ted McMahon, Ken & Beth Mock, Beth Naczkowski, Peter Pereira & Dean Allan, Catherine Roth, Stephen Rutledge & R. Rolfe, Julie Rosten, Steve & Martha Salta, Mary Starkebaum, Peter Strong, Herman Summers, Andrew Torrez, William Traver, Kris Tussey, Veruska Vagen, Vetri International Glass, Gladys & John Vordahl, Carl Walesa, Raleigh Watts & Scott LaMontagne, Debra Westwood, Gary Winans, John Zmolek & Jerry Jutting

The printing of this book was also supported by:

King County Arts Commission
&
Allied Arts Foundation

JEFF CRANDALL

Jeff Crandall is a poet and artist living in Seattle. He earned his Bachelor of Arts in Creative Writing from the University of Washington. He was a finalist in the 1994 National Poetry Series, and his poetry has appeared in numerous literary journals. His artwork combines poetic text with glass, and is featured in fine galleries throughout the United States. He volunteers as an editor at Floating Bridge Press.